Original title:
The Warm Horizon

Copyright © 2024 Swan Charm
All rights reserved.

Author: Mirell Mesipuu
ISBN HARDBACK: 978-9908-1-2719-4
ISBN PAPERBACK: 978-9908-1-2720-0
ISBN EBOOK: 978-9908-1-2721-7

Twilight's Bloom

In the hush of fading light,
Shadows stretch, take flight.
Colors blend, soft and bright,
Whispers hum, day turns night.

Petals close in twilight's grasp,
Nature sighs a gentle gasp.
Stars peek through the velvet seam,
Night unfolds like a dream.

Breezes dance with scented air,
Every moment, magic rare.
Crickets sing their evening tune,
Underneath the watchful moon.

Silhouettes of trees stand tall,
Guardians of the night's soft call.
Fireflies twinkle, warm and bright,
A chorus sings the end of light.

In this realm where shadows play,
Life and dreams softly sway.
Twilight's bloom, a fleeting joy,
Nature's peace, no need to toy.

An Offering of Light

From the heart, a glow ignites,
Shining through the darkest nights.
With each breath, hope takes its flight,
An offering of purest light.

Gentle hands reach out to guide,
Breaking barriers, turning tide.
In the warmth, all fears collide,
Together, here we will abide.

Candles flicker, spirits soar,
Echoing love forevermore.
In every shadow, whispers score,
The promise of what we explore.

Gathered close, we share our dreams,
Illuminated by moonbeams.
Life unfolds in sacred themes,
Bound together by our streams.

In this moment, hearts unite,
Shining brighter, burning bright.
An offering to hold us tight,
Together, we embrace the light.

A Soft Palette of Dreams

Whispers float on cotton clouds,
As colors blend in gentle shrouds.
A canvas draped in twilight hues,
Where every heart can freely choose.

Brush strokes of hope in pastel skies,
As moonlit thoughts begin to rise.
A symphony of hues so sweet,
Where day and night in harmony meet.

From Dusk to Dawn

The sun dips low, the shadows tease,
Night unfolds with a silent breeze.
Stars ignite in the velvety dark,
Each one a note in the night's sweet arc.

Whispers of winds tell stories true,
Of dreams that dance in the hidden blue.
Time drifts on, a soft embrace,
From dusk to dawn, a sacred space.

Murmurs of the Evenlight

Soft whispers echo through the trees,
As twilight stirs a gentle breeze.
The world holds its breath in still delight,
Embraced by the glow of evenlight.

Shadows lengthen, secrets unwind,
In the soft glow, peace we find.
Each fleeting moment, a tender thrill,
As day gives way to night's sweet chill.

When Sunlight Kisses Earth

Golden rays weave through the leaves,
A quiet warmth the heart believes.
Each touch a promise, soft and bright,
When sunlight kisses earth, pure light.

Flowers bloom in radiant cheer,
As nature whispers, calm and clear.
With every dawn, love's dance begins,
In this embrace, our joy therein.

Aglow at Dusk

The sky ignites with amber light,
Whispers of calm as day takes flight.
Shadows stretch and dance around,
As twilight's glow begins to sound.

Fireflies flicker in the eve,
Nature's magic weaves and weaves.
A starscape blooms, a velvet hue,
In this moment, dreams come true.

Silhouettes of trees stand tall,
Guardians of dusk, they watch all.
Cool breezes wrap the fading day,
In this hour, all worries sway.

Hearts connect beneath the sky,
Underneath the hues, we sigh.
The world slows down, time drips sweet,
In these moments, life feels complete.

As the sun bows low in grace,
The night brings us to a soft embrace.
Aglow at dusk, we find our peace,
In silence, all our troubles cease.

The Horizon's Glow

Beyond the edge where earth meets sky,
Dreams are painted, bright and spry.
Golden rays stretch wide and free,
A promise blooms, just wait and see.

The ocean mirrors the sun's embrace,
Ripples dance in a liquid space.
Colors swirl like laughter's sound,
In this canvas, hope is found.

Mountains stand as sentinels bold,
Guarding the stories yet untold.
With every dawn, new paths unfold,
Under the horizon's glow of gold.

In the distance, the future calls,
Echoes of laughter within the walls.
Each sunrise whispers of what's to come,
In every heart, a beating drum.

So chase the light that strokes the dusk,
Hold onto dreams, oh, hold them close.
The horizon's glow shines bright and true,
In every heartbeat, it calls to you.

Luminous Beginnings

In the dawn where shadows fade,
New hopes weave the day they've made.
Gentle light spills across the land,
Each ray a promise, soft and grand.

Buds awaken, stretch, and sway,
Colors burst in bright display.
Every moment, a chance to grow,
In luminous beginnings, we sow.

The murmur of the waking breeze,
Carries whispers through the trees.
Each heartbeat is a chance to rise,
Underneath these endless skies.

As the day breaks fresh and pure,
We find the strength to endure.
With open hearts and eyes anew,
Luminous beginnings call to you.

The world unfolds, our stories start,
A tapestry woven, heart to heart.
In every dawn, a spark ignites,
In luminous beginnings, life delights.

Hues of Hope

In the twilight, colors blend,
Whispers of peace begin to mend.
Soft pastels fill the evening air,
Hues of hope, everywhere.

Each stroke of light a gentle plea,
A reminder of what could be.
In every shade, a story sings,
The comfort that tomorrow brings.

With every breath, we hold the night,
Guided by the soft, warm light.
Fear dissolves like misty veils,
In the hues of hope, love prevails.

Stars appear like scattered dreams,
In the stillness, nothing's as it seems.
We gather strength within these tones,
In the colors, we find our homes.

As day succumbs to evening's grace,
Every moment finds its place.
In hues of hope, our hearts embrace,
The beauty of this sacred space.

Where Light Meets Earth

In the dawn's soft embrace,
Shadows dance in the morn,
Whispers of light trace,
A new day is born.

Beneath the azure skies,
Colors wake from their sleep,
Nature's breath, sweet sighs,
In harmony, we leap.

Mountains glow with grace,
Fields shimmer in the sun,
Life finds its own pace,
In beauty, we are one.

Rivers sing to the flow,
Trees sway with gentle ease,
In this tranquil show,
Hearts find their inner peace.

As day gives way to night,
Stars twinkle from above,
In the fading light,
We gather dreams of love.

Gentle Awakening

Morning dew on the grass,
The world begins to wake,
Birds chirp as they pass,
A fresh start we take.

Sunrise paints the sky,
Gold and pink gently blend,
Nature's lullaby,
On this we depend.

Soft whispers of breeze,
Caress the sleepy trees,
In this moment, ease,
Hearts float like the leaves.

Flowers bloom with grace,
Their colors rich and bright,
In this sacred space,
We bathe in pure light.

As the day unfolds,
Hope rises with the sun,
In stories retold,
A new journey's begun.

Serene Sunsets

As daylight starts to fade,
Colors fiercely collide,
In beauty we wade,
In change, we take pride.

Golden hues touch the sea,
Whispers of warmth remain,
In this tranquil plea,
We let go of the strain.

Clouds drift soft and slow,
Painting tales in the sky,
In the evening glow,
All worries say goodbye.

Night beckons with its song,
The stars begin to gleam,
In the quiet, we long,
To drift into a dream.

With each sunset we find,
Peace in the fading light,
Hearts open and kind,
As we embrace the night.

Golden Veil

In the fields of pure gold,
Waves dance in the breeze,
Stories of old unfold,
Beneath the whispering trees.

Sunlight drapes the land,
A soft and warm embrace,
Nature's gentle hand,
Fills the heart with grace.

Every petal aglow,
And skies painted bright,
In this verdant show,
All shadows take flight.

Golden hours so sweet,
Embrace the day's end,
With nature, we meet,
And love, we extend.

As dusk weaves its veil,
And stars begin to sing,
In this sacred trail,
Our souls take to wing.

Horizon's Gentle Caress

The sun kisses earth goodnight,
Painting skies with hues of gold.
Waves whisper secrets to the shore,
Underneath the stars, dreams unfold.

Mountains stand tall in silence,
Guardians of tales untold.
As the twilight breathes softly,
Night's embrace—warm and bold.

Birds find rest in hidden nests,
While the moon begins to rise.
A soft glow spills through the trees,
Embracing the night's gentle sighs.

The horizon fades into dreams,
Where shadows play and dance.
A canvas of starlit wishes,
With every glance—a new chance.

Night deepens, wrapping the world,
In a cloak of tranquil grace.
Horizon's gentle caress remains,
Sweet comfort in this sacred space.

Dawn's Promise

The night retreats, a silent thief,
As dawn unfolds her vibrant wings.
Whispers of light paint the world,
And with it, the hope of new beginnings.

Birds herald the day's arrival,
With songs that flutter through the mist.
Gentle sunlight warms the earth,
For every soul to coexist.

Buds bloom in a symphony,
Their colors bright against the dew.
Nature stirs from restful slumber,
Awakening to life anew.

The sky blushes in shades of pink,
Clouds float like dreams in the expanse.
With each ray, a silent promise,
Inviting all to join the dance.

As shadows flee before the light,
A canvas fresh, untouched by time.
Dawn's promise lingers in the air,
A reminder that life can shine.

Evening's Soft Breath

Evening drapes a silken veil,
As the sun dips low with grace.
Colors blend and shadows merge,
In the hush of twilight's embrace.

The world slows its hurried pace,
Whispers float like petals in air.
Crickets sing of summer nights,
Under the watch of the moon's glare.

Stars sprinkle the evening sky,
A tapestry of glimmering dreams.
Each one tells a story bright,
In the web of night, love redeems.

The breeze carries scents of calm,
Rustling leaves in gentle sway.
Evening's soft breath caresses skin,
Inviting hearts to pause and stay.

As darkness deepens, peace descends,
Cradling the earth in quiet rest.
In the arms of the night, we find,
A haven where our souls are blessed.

A Symphony of Colors

In gardens where the flowers bloom,
A symphony of colors thrives.
Petals dance in the gentle wind,
Each shade sings, each moment drives.

Lavender hues kiss the sunset,
While daisies wave their bright heads high.
Greens brush against warm sunlight,
As butterflies twirl in the sky.

Reds ignite the horizon's edge,
A passionate blaze, a fervent plea.
Golden rays filter through branches,
Creating magic, wild and free.

A painter's palette spills delight,
In every corner, life ignites.
Nature's canvas, bold and bright,
Offers solace in shared sights.

And as day bows to the night,
Colors fade, but hearts remain.
A symphony that echoes still,
In memories, joy's sweet refrain.

Sunlit Whispers

In the dawn's soft light,
Whispers dance in the breeze,
Gentle kisses of gold,
Awakening the trees.

Petals open wide,
To greet the morning's song,
Nature's sweet embrace,
Where all hearts belong.

Through the shimmering leaves,
Sunbeams play and twirl,
Creating fleeting dreams,
In a bright, warm swirl.

Children laugh and run,
Chasing shadows of joy,
Every moment cherished,
In this world, they employ.

As the day unfolds,
Moments gently fade,
Sunlit whispers linger,
In memories we've made.

Ember Skies

As daylight softly wanes,
Embers light the night,
Rust and crimson splashes,
Creating pure delight.

Stars peek through the veil,
Whispers of the past,
Each twinkle tells a tale,
Of shadows that we cast.

The moon a silver coin,
In an azure sea,
Glows upon the silent,
As it watches me.

Night blooms like a flower,
In the cool, crisp air,
Dreams begin to dance,
With a tender flair.

Ember skies above,
Holding secrets tight,
Guiding our thoughts home,
Through the endless night.

A Tapestry of Glow

In the fabric of dusk,
Colors start to blend,
Threads of deep indigo,
With a soft gold mend.

Waves of vibrant light,
Cascade through the trees,
Painting hearts with warmth,
And a gentle breeze.

Each moment unfolds,
Like a story untold,
Woven in the stars,
And the air, so bold.

A canvas of dreams,
Bathed in twilight's hue,
Every heart beats close,
With a love that feels true.

In this tapestry,
Life's beauty aligns,
Glowing bright with hope,
Through infinite signs.

Luminous Reverie

In the quiet night sky,
Dreams begin to sway,
A luminous reverie,
Guiding hearts to play.

Soft whispers of light,
Echo through the stars,
Inviting every spirit,
To reach for what's ours.

With every pulse of hope,
Shadows start to flee,
Illuminated pathways,
Leading us to see.

Voices of the unseen,
Crafting tales so bright,
A dance of endless wonder,
Filling up the night.

In this wondrous dream,
Magic starts to gleam,
Luminous reverie,
Is more than it seems.

The Dance of Day and Night

Daylight stretches wide and bright,
Painting skies with golden light.
Night descends with stars aglow,
In shadows deep where dreams can flow.

Sunrise whispers soft and sweet,
While shadows sway to rhythm's beat.
Twilight blends both dark and light,
In the dance of day and night.

Resplendent Veil

Morning drapes in hues of rose,
Softly where the wild wind blows.
Evening glistens with a tear,
A resplendent veil appears.

Underneath the heavens vast,
Wonder fades, but hopes hold fast.
Every star a wish unfurls,
Casting light on dreaming worlds.

A Canvas of Fire

Leaves ablaze in autumn's breath,
Nature's brush speaks life and death.
Every hue a story shared,
In the flames that we have dared.

Crimson skies at dusk's warm kiss,
A whispered touch, a fleeting bliss.
Each moment framed in fleeting time,
A canvas of fire, so sublime.

Horizon's Tender Grasp

The horizon holds a gentle sway,
Between the dusk and the break of day.
Whispers float on the evening breeze,
A tender grasp that aims to please.

Waves of light and silhouette dance,
To the rhythm of fate and chance.
In the distance, dreams emerge,
As the world's heart begins to surge.

A Twilight Tapestry

The sun dips low, painting the sky,
Shadows stretch long, as the day says goodbye.
Whispers of dusk dance in the breeze,
Nature's embrace, a gentle tease.

Stars begin to twinkle, one by one,
Night's soft cloak wraps around everyone.
Colors blend in a silky hue,
A tapestry woven, rich and true.

Silhouettes mingle in fading light,
Dreams awaken to the whispers of night.
The world slows down, in peace it dwells,
As silence sings its soothing spells.

From day to night, a seamless turn,
In every heart, a flicker that burns.
Time ebbs gently, the sky's embrace,
In twilight's grasp, we find our place.

Flickering Promises

In the shadows, promises lie,
Flickering softly like stars in the sky.
Whispers of hope on the cool night air,
Binding our souls in a silent prayer.

Moments of magic, like fireflies' glow,
Carrying dreams as we ebb and flow.
Paths intertwined, our futures aligned,
In this dance of fate, our hearts defined.

The glow of our laughter breaks through the dark,
Creating a canvas, a vibrant mark.
With each flicker, a new tale begins,
In the warmth of the light, our love never thins.

Catch the sparks as they rise and fall,
Echoes of laughter, a radiant call.
In flickering promises, we'll find our way,
Bound by the rhythm of night and day.

Pathway of Radiance

A pathway of radiance unfolds at dawn,
Golden hues shimmer, casting light on the lawn.
Each step forward, a song in our feet,
With whispers of hope that life is sweet.

The brush of soft petals, a fragrant embrace,
Guiding us gently through this magical space.
Sunbeams cascade, warming our skin,
In the heart of the moment, new journeys begin.

Through shadows and light, we navigate still,
Fueled by the fire of our unwavering will.
The beauty around us, a constant thread,
Weaving our dreams into blueprints ahead.

Embracing the day with a smile so bright,
In the pathway of radiance, our spirits take flight.
Every step taken, a dance of delight,
Guided by love, we soar to new heights.

Starlit Echoes

In the midnight hour, starlit echoes play,
Whispers of the cosmos, leading the way.
Each twinkle a story, a memory kept,
In the silence of night, our secrets are swept.

Dreams drift like clouds in the vast velvet sky,
Fleeting moments of time gently pass by.
Under the blanket where wishes ignite,
We find our reflections in the depths of night.

The moon casts shadows, a silvered embrace,
Illuminating paths, revealing our grace.
Amongst the stars, our hopes take their flight,
In starlit echoes, we feel infinite light.

As dawn approaches, the magic will fade,
But in our hearts, the night will remain.
With starlit echoes, we'll never be lost,
For in every moment, there's beauty embossed.

Shadows of Radiance

In twilight's grasp, soft whispers play,
Where shadows dance and light decays,
A fleeting glimpse of what once shone,
In echoes past, we stand alone.

Glistening dreams on a silken thread,
Woven tales of the sun once bled,
With every heartbeat, time unfolds,
The stories lost, the shadows told.

Beneath the stars, a silent sigh,
As night brings forth the lullaby,
Of memories framed in silver light,
The shadows rise, embracing night.

Through emerald leaves, the night winds weep,
In darkness deep, our secrets keep,
With every breath, the shadows blend,
A radiant glow we can't defend.

With every flicker, the dusk extends,
A light that dims, yet never ends,
In shadows' arms, we find our way,
To the dawn that whispers, come and play.

Embracing the Nightfall

As daylight fades, the colors wane,
The night wraps close, a velvet chain,
Beneath the moon's soft, silver gleam,
We find ourselves in endless dream.

The stars awaken, bright and bold,
Their tales of love and loss retold,
In the embrace of night so grand,
We grasp the magic at our hand.

With every shadow drawn, we sigh,
For in the dark, our hopes can fly,
A tranquil heart, a silent song,
To night's allure, we all belong.

In quiet corners, secrets weave,
Through whispering winds, we dare believe,
That every shadow hides a spark,
To guide us home when days grow dark.

So, let us dance till stars align,
And weave our dreams through night's design,
For in the dusk, our spirits twine,
Embracing nightfall, hearts entwined.

Melodies of the Dying Light

As sunset paints the world in gold,
A symphony of tales unfolds,
With every hue, a story flies,
The melodies that touch the skies.

As day concedes to twilight's grace,
We find our rhythm in the space,
Where shadows stretch and whispers rise,
A serenade of soft goodbyes.

The fading light, a gentle kiss,
It wraps our dreams in tender bliss,
While stars awaken, dreams take flight,
In harmony of day and night.

Each moment lingers, sweetly bound,
In fading glow, our hearts resound,
For every note, a life we trace,
In melodies, we find our place.

So let the twilight sing its song,
In dying light, we still belong,
For every end gives way to start,
The music lingers in our heart.

The Fading Glow

Once vibrant flames that brightly burned,
In gentle hues, the daylight turned,
A fading glow, a whispered sigh,
In dusk's embrace, we learn to fly.

With every flicker, the shadows rise,
As evening drapes the azure skies,
In twilight's hush, our hopes renew,
The fading glow, a light so true.

The echoes of the day retreat,
In soft caress, our hearts we meet,
Through veils of dusk, our spirits roam,
In fading glow, we find our home.

As stars emerge, the world transforms,
In cosmic dances, love informs,
With every breath, we feel the flow,
Of time's embrace, the fading glow.

So let us gather, hand in hand,
In twilight's glow, we take our stand,
With every heartbeat, dreams will grow,
Together strong, in fading glow.

Sundrenched Pathways

Golden rays spill down,
A path of warmth and light,
Whispers dance in leaves,
The day holds pure delight.

Soft shadows gently creep,
Beneath the tall green trees,
Footsteps echo lightly,
In the sweet, summer breeze.

Fields of daisies sway,
Colors bright and alive,
Nature's song surrounds,
As the heart starts to thrive.

Winding trails ahead,
Adventures sweetly call,
A journey through the sun,
Embracing one and all.

With each step I take,
Hope blossoms in the air,
Sundrenched pathways lead,
To moments rich and rare.

Seasons of Warmth

When spring begins to bloom,
Life awakens anew,
Colors burst and blend,
In skies of perfect blue.

Summer brings a glow,
Days languid and bright,
Laughter fills the air,
As hearts drift with delight.

Autumn's crisp embrace,
Leaves dance in gold and rust,
A tapestry of change,
In nature we trust.

Winter whispers soft,
With blankets made of white,
Crackling fireside tales,
Warmth in the chilly night.

Through each passing cycle,
Life's rhythm finds its place,
In seasons of warmth,
We cherish each embrace.

Blossoming Light

In gardens filled with hope,
Petals gently unfold,
Each bloom tells a story,
Of love and joys untold.

Morning dew like jewels,
Glistens on the green,
Every ray of sunshine,
Makes the world serene.

Bees hum their sweet tune,
Dancing from flower to flower,
Nature's vibrant song,
Celebrating each hour.

As twilight draws near,
Colors fade to soft night,
Yet in every shadow,
Lies a blossoming light.

For even in darkness,
Hope's glow will remain,
Guiding hearts ever close,
Through sunshine and rain.

Embered Reflections

Flickers dance in the dark,
Soft warmth against the chill,
Memories rise like smoke,
A calmness, a thrill.

Gathered 'round the fire,
Stories shared and spun,
Each ember holds a dream,
Warming everyone.

Crisp autumn leaves fall,
Underneath a blanket sky,
Moments pause in stillness,
As time drifts gently by.

The crackling of the wood,
A symphony of night,
In the heart of the world,
Embers glowing bright.

These reflections of time,
In warmth and gentle light,
Remind us to hold close,
What makes our spirits light.

The Light Beyond

In shadows deep, I seek the glow,
A distant warmth, a softening flow.
With every step, the dark retreats,
Illuminating paths, where hope meets.

Flickering flames dance in the night,
Guiding souls to the brink of light.
Each whisper calls from beyond the veil,
A promise kept, a lover's tale.

Amidst the stars, a beacon shines,
Breaking the bonds of earthly signs.
Eternal glimmers on the rise,
A sight that lifts, a sweet surprise.

The world awakens, colors gleam,
In light's embrace, we find our dream.
Together we chase, hand in hand,
Into the dawn, a promised land.

So let us wander, unafraid,
Through realms where shadows softly fade.
With hearts aflame, and spirits free,
We'll find the light, just you and me.

Celestial Caress

A touch of stars across the skies,
Whispers of night, where silence lies.
Cosmic winds, they gently sweep,
In their embrace, the world feels deep.

Moonlit dreams on velvet sheets,
Twirling thoughts in rhythmic beats.
Every breath a sacred dance,
In the stillness, souls enhance.

Galaxies twirl in graceful grace,
Embracing all in a warm embrace.
The universe hums a timeless song,
In this vastness, we all belong.

With stardust crowns, we rise and soar,
To heights unseen, forevermore.
Hand in hand, we touch the divine,
In celestial love, our hearts align.

So let us drift through cosmic seas,
Beneath the constellations' breeze.
A gentle caress from up above,
In the space of dreams, we find our love.

Awakening Beams

Morning dew on petals bright,
Whispers dawn with pure delight.
Beams of gold stretch across the land,
Gift of life, a gentle hand.

As daylight graces every tree,
Nature wakes, so wild and free.
Birds take flight on sunlit wings,
In their songs, the morning sings.

Colors burst, the canvas wide,
A masterpiece where dreams abide.
Each moment blooms, a fleeting grace,
In the warmth, we find our place.

The world ignites in vibrant hues,
Awakening hearts to life's renews.
As shadows fade, the light expands,
Together we walk on golden sands.

So take my hand, let's journey far,
In this magic, you are my star.
With every dawn, our spirits lift,
Awakening beams, a precious gift.

Colorful Reverie

In a garden where dreams collide,
Petals dance, and colors glide.
Brush of nature, soft and fair,
Each hue whispers of love and care.

Crimson skies at twilight's birth,
Painting wonders, a canvas of earth.
Golden rays through emerald leaves,
In nature's heart, the soul believes.

Gentle breezes carry song,
In this reverie, we belong.
Twilight hues blend and sway,
Time stands still, as night greets day.

A tapestry of passions bright,
In every shadow, a spark of light.
With open eyes, we'll chase our dreams,
In life's grand stage, nothing is as it seems.

So let us wander, hand in hand,
Through fields of dreams, across the land.
In this colorful tapestry, we're free,
Living our vibrant reverie.

Moments Between Hours

In the quiet of the dusk,
Whispers drift through the air.
Time bends in fragile shards,
Caught in a fleeting stare.

A breath held in stillness,
As shadows dance on the wall.
Each second stretches onward,
Echoes faintly call.

Fleeting thoughts like whispers,
In the close of day's light.
We linger in silence,
Chasing dreams into night.

Soft laughter fills the spaces,
Where memories intertwine.
Each moment shared is sacred,
A treasure, sweet and fine.

So here between the hours,
We hold what's pure and true,
In the heart of twilight,
I find my peace with you.

Dayspring of Promise

The dawn breaks softly bright,
Colors spill from the skies.
Hope unfurls its bright wings,
With each new day's surprise.

A whispering breeze calls forth,
As petals greet the sun.
Every heartbeat carries dreams,
A new beginning's run.

Through fields of golden light,
Seasons whisper their song.
In the dayspring of promise,
Each moment feels so strong.

Amidst the dew-kissed grass,
Life awakens to play.
With each step towards the future,
We dance the dawn away.

In the glow of the morning,
We find our strength and grace.
Together, hand in hand,
We journey, face to face.

Horizon's Last Embrace

As the sun dips low,
The horizon blushes fair.
Crimson hues caress the sky,
In evening's gentle care.

A moment rich with silence,
Where shadows start to grow.
Stars emerge like whispers,
In twilight's softening glow.

The world holds its breath now,
In the stillness of time.
Memories weave like stars,
In patterns so sublime.

Each heartbeat echoes softly,
As darkness finds its place.
In the horizon's last embrace,
I feel your warm grace.

So let us cherish this hour,
As day yields to the night.
For in each fleeting moment,
Our souls take flight.

The Glow Before Dusk

In the stillness of the eve,
A golden light appears.
The world shimmers and sighs,
As daylight slowly clears.

Gentle whispers of the night,
Begin to softly hum.
Crickets play their lullabies,
As twilight is now come.

The trees sway with secrets kept,
In shadows deep and wide.
Each moment is a treasure,
As day and night collide.

With every breath, we gather,
The fading warmth of time.
In the glow before dusk falls,
We find our hearts in rhyme.

So let us pause together,
And savor this soft light.
For in the glow of the evening,
All worries fade from sight.

Golden Horizons

The sun dipped low, a fiery glow,
Waves danced gently, a soft hello.
Golden light kissed the land,
A moment perfect, forever stand.

Birds took flight, silhouettes bold,
Stories of freedom, yet untold.
An evening calm, whispers of peace,
In nature's arms, our worries cease.

Fields of amber, swaying slow,
Breeze carries secrets, as it flows.
Each petal glistens, a radiant sight,
In the fading warmth of soft twilight.

With every breath, the beauty swells,
Tales of wonder, nature tells.
As stars emerge, the night awakes,
Every moment, a treasure breaks.

Golden horizons, dreams unfold,
Captured memories, stories told.
In heart's embrace, we find our way,
Guided always by the light of day.

Chasing the Sun

On misty morns, we rise with glee,
The sun's first rays, a sight to see.
We wander far, our spirits high,
Chasing shadows as they fly.

Through golden fields, our laughter spills,
Beyond the hills, over the thrills.
In every heartbeat, joy we find,
With open hearts and curious minds.

The sunbeams dance on dew-kissed grass,
Moments fleeting, yet they last.
With every step, we feel alive,
In nature's rhythm, we thrive.

The horizon beckons, wild and free,
Where sky meets earth, eternally.
Chasing dreams as day unfolds,
A journey written in hues of gold.

As the sun dips low, we gather round,
Sharing stories, laughter, sound.
In twilight's glow, we find our peace,
In chasing the sun, our joys increase.

Flickers of Dawn's Magic

In the hush of dawn, whispers arise,
The world awakens under gentle skies.
Soft hues blend in a dreamy trance,
Nature's peformance, a sweet dance.

Birds begin their morning song,
In perfect harmony, where we belong.
A canvas painted in shades of rose,
Where every heartbeat gently flows.

Dewdrops glisten on emerald leaves,
A moment captured that the heart believes.
Amidst the stillness, magic ignites,
Flickers of hope in morning lights.

As shadows retreat and daylight breaks,
Awakening spirits in the still lakes.
With every breath, a promise new,
In the dawn's embrace, dreams come true.

Through fleeting moments, we find our way,
In the soul's melody, come what may.
Flickers of dawn, a gift divine,
With every sunrise, our hearts align.

Sublime Skies

The azure expanse, vast and bright,
Clouds drifting softly, pure delight.
Colors collide in perfect embrace,
A celestial canvas, a tranquil space.

From dawn to dusk, moods shift and sway,
Sun-kissed mornings chase clouds away.
As twilight descends, stars start to gleam,
In sublime skies, we dare to dream.

Whispers of wind carry tales untold,
In every sunset, mysteries unfold.
The moon takes her throne, silver and wise,
In the quietude, we hear her sighs.

Beneath this expanse, we stand in awe,
Nature's beauty, without a flaw.
In every glance, we find our muse,
In sublime skies, our hearts choose.

So let us wander, hand in hand,
Through skies adorned, so vast, so grand.
In every moment, life's wonder lies,
Together we soar, beneath sublime skies.

Day's Last Breath

The sun dips low in the sky,
Whispers of night starting to sigh.
Shadows stretch and begin to cling,
While the world prepares for evening's fling.

Colors blend in a soft embrace,
Golden hues in fading grace.
A gentle breeze carries a song,
Echoing where dreams belong.

Clouds painted in fiery red,
As daylight softly retreats to bed.
The stars awaken, one by one,
Bidding farewell to the day that's done.

Crickets chirp their lullabies,
Underneath the twilight skies.
The moon peeks through a veil of mist,
In the night, the day's last kiss.

Time flows on, the day is spent,
In the hush, sweet moments lent.
Silent promises linger near,
As night wraps all in love austere.

Sunset's Lullaby

The horizon blushes, a tender sight,
Fading away, embracing night.
Crimson waves dance in the breeze,
As daylight bows with gentle ease.

Whispers of twilight softly spread,
Painting the world in hues of red.
Nature hums a soothing tune,
Lulling the stars to wake up soon.

The sky ignites with colors bright,
A breathtaking end to the light.
Waves of warmth in the cooling air,
Sunset's grace beyond compare.

Birds return to their cozy nests,
Leaving behind the day's sweet quests.
An evening sigh, a tranquil sigh,
As the sun bids its last goodbye.

In this moment, hearts align,
To witness magic, pure and divine.
Hand in hand, as shadows call,
We find peace, embracing it all.

Dreams on the Edge of Day

Morning whispers in soft light,
Tales of dreams that take to flight.
Fleeting thoughts in the dawn's embrace,
Awakening hope, a new-found grace.

Golden rays kiss the sleepy land,
As visions weave like grains of sand.
Colors bloom on a canvas wide,
While gentle breezes tenderly guide.

The edges of day blur and blend,
In a world where time can bend.
Each heartbeat carries a secret song,
In this space where we all belong.

Laughter dances on morning's dew,
Dreams brush lightly against the blue.
As the sun climbs high in the sky,
We're reminded of wings, ready to fly.

With every moment bright and clear,
We savor whispers that draw near.
In the folds of the waking day,
Dreams await, eager to play.

Harvesting Sunbeams

In fields where golden grains do sway,
We gather sunbeams at the break of day.
Baskets full, with laughter shared,
Nature's bounty, touched and cared.

Gentle hands work through warm earth,
Nurturing life and celebrating birth.
In each seed sown, a promise waits,
As the sun casts light on our fates.

The air is thick with summer's breath,
Waves of heat, a dance with depth.
Harvest moons could cast their glow,
Yet in sunlight, our spirits grow.

Every grain tells a story old,
Of toil and joy, of dreams bold.
We reap the rays of each sunbeam,
In the heart of nature's gleam.

As twilight deepens, we'll rejoice,
With grateful hearts, we lift our voice.
In the embrace of evening's calm,
Sunbeams linger, a lasting balm.

Between Day and Night

The sunset drapes the sky in gold,
Whispers of twilight, secrets untold.
Stars begin to blink with grace,
As shadows dance in their embrace.

A gentle hush falls on the ground,
Nature's chorus, a soothing sound.
Crickets chirp, their songs take flight,
In the serene passage of night.

Dreams awaken in the dusk,
Among the leaves, a tender musk.
The world glimmers, soft and bright,
Caught in the magic between day and night.

Moonlight bathes the earth in peace,
Time slows down, the heart's release.
A moment caught in fleeting sight,
Where day concedes to the coming night.

Waves of calm wash over me,
Beneath the sky, so wild and free.
In this realm, all feels just right,
Hovering softly between day and night.

Requiem of Sunshine

A final bow, the sun retreats,
Casting shadows, the day depletes.
Mountains wear a cloak of dusk,
Nature sighs, a fleeting husk.

The golden rays find their farewell,
In softening hues, the stories swell.
Clouds embrace the sinking sphere,
In silence deep, we hold it dear.

Whispers of warmth linger long,
In the heart where memories throng.
The day may fade, but spirits rise,
In twilight's song, our laughter lies.

The echo of a vibrant morn,
Remains within, though we feel worn.
We gather light from days gone by,
In every tear, in every sigh.

As night unfurls her velvet cloak,
We cherish that which time bespoke.
A requiem for sun's bright cheer,
In shadows cast, its warmth stays near.

Infinite Echoes of Light

A shimmering pulse, a distant star,
Whispers of worlds that seem so far.
In cosmic dance, the night ignites,
Infinite echoes of radiant lights.

A spectrum blooms beyond the sky,
Painting dreams that soar and fly.
Time's soft hand reaches through the dark,
Illuminating shadows that leave a mark.

Galaxies spin in silent grace,
Each one holds a forgotten place.
Echoes linger, the past takes flight,
Journeying through the realm of light.

Every shimmer, a tale once told,
In the tapestry of stars, we behold.
Threads of history intertwine,
In the vast expanse, a hidden line.

As dawn approaches, dreams take flight,
Carried by the breath of night.
A promise written in the starlight's height,
Infinite echoes, forever bright.

Aetherial Flicker

In the quiet, a flicker glows,
Threads of magic, the soft wind blows.
A dance of spark in the night's embrace,
Nature whispers in a sacred space.

With each spark, the darkness sways,
Holding secrets of forgotten days.
Through the veil of silence, it twirls,
Aetherial light, a story unfurls.

Fleeting moments, caught in the air,
Hints of wonder, free from care.
A tender pulse, so soft, so swift,
In the night's silk, we find our gift.

With stardust dreams that intertwine,
The world awakens, pure and divine.
Each flicker a promise, bold and bright,
Guiding our hearts through the magical night.

So let us chase that whimsical glow,
Follow the paths where the dreamers go.
In the realm where shadows flicker,
We find our truth in the aetherial sticker.

Daybreak's Parenthesis

In morning's hush, the world awakes,
A canvas bright, where silence breaks.
Soft hues paint the sky anew,
As night retreats, the day breaks through.

Birdsong weaves through golden air,
Each note a promise, light and rare.
The dew-kissed grass glimmers and glows,
While warmth of sun begins to flow.

Shadows stretch, a playful dance,
Inviting all to take a chance.
With every breath, the moment swells,
In daybreak's arms, the spirit dwells.

Clouds drift lazily, trails of white,
Framing the canvas, soft and bright.
As laughter springs from hearts set free,
Each sunrise holds a mystery.

With open arms, we greet the dawn,
In daybreak's light, our fears are gone.
Each moment spins a tale so grand,
Where hope and love forever stand.

Whisper of the Dawn

A gentle breeze through branches weaves,
The dawn's soft whisper, nature grieves.
In stillness held, the world takes breath,
A quiet pause before the quest.

Birds unfurl their wings to fly,
In pastel skies where dreams comply.
The sun peeks out, a golden ray,
Awakening life in the clay.

Each moment brief, a treasure found,
In shadows cast upon the ground.
Awareness blooms where hearts align,
In dawn's embrace, we feel divine.

The earth exhales a fragrant sigh,
As day unfolds, no need to try.
With every pulse, a sacred rite,
The whisper lingers in the light.

In this still hour, let love expand,
As dawn invites us, hand in hand.
We'll dance beneath the stretching beams,
Embracing life and all its dreams.

Light's Gentle Caress

Softly creeping, light descends,
A tender touch that never ends.
It kisses petals, fresh and bright,
And bathes the world in pure delight.

With every ray, the heart ignites,
As shadows wane and spirit takes flight.
A golden glow that warms the soul,
In light's embrace, we find our goal.

The morning's blush brings peace anew,
As whispers weave through fields of dew.
In every corner, joy resides,
As light reveals what love abides.

Sunbeams dance on rippling streams,
In nature's quiet, endless dreams.
Where earth and sky in colors blend,
Light's gentle touch, our faithful friend.

Let every heart be open wide,
And bask in warmth, let love abide.
For in the light, we truly see,
The beauty in our tapestry.

Crocus in the Sun

Tiny blooms where snow once lay,
Crocus peeks through, bright and gay.
In sunlight's warmth, they gently rise,
A painted brush on spring's blue skies.

Their vibrant hues, a song of birth,
A promise whispered into earth.
Each petal opens, wide and free,
A fleeting glimpse of what can be.

As winter's grip begins to fade,
The crocus stands, a bold crusade.
In gardens lush, they stake their claim,
With laughter bright, they spread their fame.

Amidst the green, they claim their place,
An artist's touch, a soft embrace.
Each crocus bloom, a spark divine,
In nature's heart, our lives entwine.

So let us cherish, let us grow,
Like crocus bright, our spirits glow.
In every season's fleeting span,
We find our joy, as flowers can.

Dawn's Embrace

Soft light spills over the hills,
Awakening blooms with vibrant thrills.
A gentle breeze stirs the trees,
Nature sighs, invoking peace.

Birdsong dances on the air,
Whispers of morning everywhere.
The sky, a canvas brushed with gold,
Stories of the new day unfold.

Shadows retreat in the glow,
Radiance spreads, a warm halo.
Hope ignites in the heart's space,
Every moment, a sweet embrace.

Clouds drift slow, painted in hue,
Dreams are born, fresh and anew.
With every ray, life starts to climb,
In this dawn, we find our rhyme.

The day awakens, bright and clear,
Inviting laughter, drawing near.
With each heartbeat, the world we trace,
In the magic of Dawn's embrace.

Radiant Whispers

In twilight's glow, shadows play,
Stars emerge to light the way.
Night's gentle hush, a calming song,
As dreams awaken, where we belong.

Breeze carries secrets unspun,
Echoing tales of the moonlit run.
Whispers of love in the cool night air,
Promises linger, silent and rare.

Soft moonbeams weave through the trees,
Kissing leaves with tender ease.
In this moment, time stands still,
Hearts entwined, wrapped in thrill.

Mysteries linger, softly spoken,
In the night, no heart is broken.
Every sigh, a radiant prayer,
Binding us close, beyond compare.

As daylight fades, the stars ignite,
Radiant whispers fill the night.
In this dance of shadow and light,
Our souls unite, taking flight.

Sunlit Promise

Golden rays kiss the waking earth,
Celebrating life, a day of rebirth.
Flowers bloom with joyful grace,
Every petal, a warm embrace.

Meadows stretch beneath the sky,
Where laughter dances, spirits fly.
Hope is woven in each thread,
In sunlit promise, all is said.

The horizon glows with a fiery hue,
Bringing dreams alive, fresh and new.
Each moment sparkles, pure delight,
In the warmth of the morning light.

Flowing rivers mirror the sun,
Whispers of life, a race begun.
Every heartbeat, a soft refrain,
In this promise, love shall reign.

As daylight fades, memories bloom,
Chasing away shadows and gloom.
With every sunset, the world we find,
In sunlit promise, hearts aligned.

Embered Skies

Cinder clouds drift, tinged with flame,
Crimson whispers call your name.
The sun bows down, a spectral guide,
As dusk envelops, time does glide.

Beneath the glow of twilight's sigh,
Dreams take flight, soaring high.
Each heartbeat, a story told,
In embered skies, life unfolds.

Stars awaken, one by one,
Greeting the eve, a new day done.
Fireflies twinkle in playful trails,
Guiding our hearts with soft exhales.

Night wraps around like a cloak,
Hallowed silence mirrors the smoke.
With every pulse, the world ignites,
In embered skies, love ignites.

As shadows fall, the journey starts,
Illuminated by hopeful hearts.
Together we chase the starlit rise,
In the warmth of embered skies.

The Colors of Day's End

Golden hues in the sky,
Whispers of night draw near.
Fields bathed in soft light,
As the sun sheds a tear.

Crimson clouds float high,
Dancing with shadows long.
The world starts to sigh,
Nature sings her song.

Amber glows touch the trees,
With whispers of gentle winds.
As the day starts to freeze,
The horizon slowly bends.

Sapphire gleam of the sea,
Reflects the fading rays.
In this tranquil decree,
Time no longer stays.

Night falls with a sigh,
Stars flicker in delight.
The colors fade up high,
Embracing the coming night.

Blushing Twilight

The sky blushes soft pink,
As the sun bids farewell.
Clouds whisper and wink,
In twilight's magic spell.

Violet threads intertwine,
As day gives way to night.
Illuminated divine,
Stars prepare for their flight.

A breeze stirs the trees,
Bringing secrets untold.
With each rustling leaf,
The evening unfolds bold.

The horizon holds dreams,
In the warmth of the dusk.
Caught in twilight's beams,
Where night finds its husk.

Fading light hangs low,
As shadows take their place.
In this gentle glow,
Time softly leaves a trace.

Beacons of Serenity

Whispers of calm abound,
On this tranquil night.
Stars twinkle all around,
Guiding with gentle light.

Moonbeams kiss the lake,
As ripples start to dance.
Nature's sweet heartache,
In a serene romance.

Soft winds carry a song,
Through branches swaying free.
In this moment, we're strong,
Feeling perfect harmony.

Dreams linger in the air,
With hopes that softly soar.
In the night's gentle care,
We await what's in store.

Each heartbeat is a glow,
Echoing nature's tune.
We're wrapped in peace we know,
Underneath the full moon.

Lasting Radiance

As daylight starts to wane,
A glow begins to rise.
Painting skies in a vein,
Where shadows meet the skies.

In hues of lasting gold,
Moments intertwine,
The beauty we behold,
A true and sacred sign.

Fingers of light extend,
Reaching out to embrace.
Every sorrow we mend,
In this warm, gentle space.

Soft laughter in the air,
Brings light to the heart.
Memories learned with care,
In this arcane art.

As the sun bids adieu,
The stars begin to gleam.
With dreams that feel so true,
We cherish night's sweet beam.

A Horizon Wreathed in Gold

The sun dips low, a soft embrace,
Casting shadows on the silent place.
Whispers of day fade into night,
As colors dance in fading light.

Fields aglow with a golden hue,
Nature's canvas, forever new.
Each moment caught in a fleeting frame,
A memory etched, a heart aflame.

Clouds painted gently, a brush of grace,
Softening edges, time's gentle pace.
Hope arises with each dawn's breath,
In golden glory, life conquers death.

Waves of light ripple through the air,
A fleeting moment, a whispered prayer.
In this visage, worries unfurl,
As the night sky begins to swirl.

A horizon wreathed in dreams untold,
Each heartbeat echoes, vibrant and bold.
We stand in awe, united, whole,
As the day bows down, enriching the soul.

Silhouettes Against the Sky

Figures dance in twilight's glow,
Eclipsed by shadows, soft and slow.
Against the sky, they weave and sway,
Painting tales before the day.

Trees stretch high, a lined embrace,
Kissing the stars with whispered grace.
Their branches cradle the setting sun,
As dusk descends, a day well-spun.

Misty whispers drift and twirl,
In this twilight, dreams unfurl.
The horizon blurs, dark and light,
A canvas born of day and night.

Laughter dances on evening's breath,
In silhouettes, a life bequeathed.
Underneath the vast expanse,
We find our peace, we find our chance.

Silhouettes against a fading sky,
A silent promise, a gentle sigh.
In moments shared, hearts intertwine,
Under the stars, your hand in mine.

Jude's Glimmer

In the quiet night, a sparkle bright,
Jude's glimmer shines, a guiding light.
Laughter trails like fireflies,
In the fabric of dreams, love never dies.

A gentle warmth, a soft embrace,
Cradled in moments we can't replace.
Through every heartbeat, the echoes sing,
In Jude's glimmer, we find everything.

Stars above, a scattered gaze,
Reflecting in eyes that softly blaze.
Together we wander, hand in hand,
In this glimmering world, we take a stand.

Whispers linger in the stillness rare,
Tales of hope dance in the air.
In the quiet places, love takes flight,
In Jude's glimmer, the world feels right.

A promise woven in stardust threads,
In every heartbeat, the journey spreads.
Together we shine, bright as the moon,
In Jude's glimmer, we find our tune.

Celestial Surrender

The night unfolds, a velvet shroud,
With whispered dreams, softly loud.
Stars flicker like forgotten tales,
In celestial dance, where wonder prevails.

Moonlight bathes the earth in grace,
A silver smile on nature's face.
In shadows deep, secrets reside,
In celestial surrender, hearts abide.

Each twinkling star, a wish sent high,
Floating gently through the vast sky.
In the silence, the heartbeats tune,
As the universe hums a gentle rune.

Cradled by night, we find our peace,
In this moment, all troubles cease.
Together we soar, on dreams we ride,
In celestial surrender, side by side.

Our souls entwined in the cosmic thread,
Through every heartbeat, love is spread.
In the starlit tapestry, we find our way,
In celestial surrender, forever we stay.

Glimmering Pathways

In the twilight's gentle glow,
The path unfolds with silver light,
Whispers of breezes softly blow,
Guiding dreams into the night.

Stars above begin to tease,
Dancing on a velvet sky,
Nature's tune, a sweet reprise,
As moonbeams laugh and softly sigh.

Footsteps echo, soft and sure,
Through the realms of shadowed haze,
Every turn, a heart's allure,
A journey lost in endless maze.

Through the dark, a glimmer gleams,
Promises of hope unfold,
Woven tightly into dreams,
Stories waiting to be told.

Hand in hand, we tread anew,
With courage lighting up our way,
Together brave, we're born to view,
This glimmering path we sway.

Celestial Embrace

Underneath the endless sky,
Constellations weave their lace,
Glimmers of a soft goodbye,
In the warmth of a celestial embrace.

Planets spin in graceful dance,
Galaxies whisper tales of old,
Caught within a timeless trance,
In the cosmos' arms, we're bold.

Stardust drifts, a gentle sigh,
Hopes entwined in silver threads,
Echoes of the evening sky,
In dreams our hearts are led.

Moments suspended, pure delight,
As the heavens align with grace,
Wrapped in love throughout the night,
Lost in a celestial embrace.

Each heartbeat, a cosmic play,
Infinite in its soft caress,
Together we will find our way,
In this starry wilderness.

Echoes of Light

In the dawn, the shadows fade,
Whispers of the morning bright,
Every hue a serenade,
Carved by echoes of the light.

Beneath the sun's warm, golden glow,
Nature dances, life takes flight,
In each blossom, secrets flow,
Voices linger, pure and bright.

Every ray a story spins,
Painting dreams in vibrant hues,
From the depths, our journey begins,
With every echo, hope renews.

Through the valleys, over hills,
Light leads us where we belong,
In the silence, a soft thrill,
In echoes, we find our song.

In the twilight, shadows play,
Yet the light remains in sight,
Guiding us along the way,
In the gentle echoes of light.

Golden Embrace

As the sun begins to set,
Fields aglow with golden sheen,
A quiet moment we shall get,
In a world that's lush and green.

With every breeze, the whispers flow,
Nature wraps us in its grace,
In this warmth, our spirits grow,
Finding strength in golden space.

Hand in hand, we share a dream,
Time stands still, just you and I,
In the glow of twilight's beam,
Where the skies and hearts comply.

Each laugh, each sigh, a tender trace,
Upon the canvas of our day,
Creating memories we embrace,
In the warmth of love's display.

As darkness falls, the stars arise,
Yet our hearts remain a blaze,
In the beauty of our eyes,
We find our peace in golden embrace.

Trail of Embered Hues

In twilight's grasp, the shadows play,
Brushstrokes of gold chase night away.
Whispers of warmth, the stars attest,
On crimson paths, the heart finds rest.

Leaves dance lightly on the breeze,
A symphony sung through rustling trees.
Echoes of fire in fading light,
Embered hues embrace the night.

Glimmers of hope on each horizon,
Every step a new season's risen.
Beneath the sky's wide canvas drawn,
A tapestry wakes with the dawn.

With every heartbeat, the colors blend,
Nature's canvas will never end.
Burnished dreams in every sigh,
Trail of embered hues in the sky.

Forever marked by sunset's tease,
A legacy sways in the gentle breeze.
The heart takes flight, the spirit roams,
In this radiant world, we find our homes.

Nurtured by Sunset

Golden rays through branches weave,
A tapestry that dusk will cleave.
The sky ignites in ripened tones,
Nature breathes as daylight moans.

Embers flicker, shadows crawl,
Whispers stir from the evening's call.
A lullaby of soft embrace,
Kissed by twilight's tender grace.

Fields drink deep the fading light,
As day surrenders to approaching night.
Crickets chirp in gentle rhyme,
Nature's heartbeat, measured time.

The horizon blazes, a child's delight,
Painting dreams in shades of night.
With every breath, we find our way,
Guided by the warmth of day.

Embers glow in our hearts' keep,
Nurtured by sunset's tender sweep.
Here in twilight, we find our tone,
In the quiet, we are never alone.

Serenading the Last Light

As day departs in softest sighs,
The sun bows low, a fond reprise.
Notes of dusk in the evening's song,
Where shadows stretch and dreams belong.

Whispers of twilight gently sweep,
From fields of gold to valleys deep.
With each chord, the night appears,
Journey woven through hopes and fears.

Last light dances on the earth,
A serenade of endless mirth.
Silhouettes in quiet pause,
Capturing grace without a cause.

The stars awaken, light the way,
While dreams ascend at close of day.
In twilight's hush, a story spun,
A testament to all we've won.

So let us toast the fading glow,
To moments cherished, hearts that know.
As night unfolds its velvet cloak,
In quietude, love's song we stoke.

Kisses of Aurora

When dawn awakens from slumber's hold,
A flush of colors, bright and bold.
Kisses of light touch earth anew,
Nature's palette in vibrant hue.

The sky ignites with a gentle blush,
As whispers of wind begin to rush.
Morning's embrace, a tender sigh,
Promises gleam in the day's first light.

Birds sing sweetly, their voices lift,
A celebration, a sacred gift.
Among the trees, sunlight breaks,
Inviting love in gentle wakes.

With every ray, the world ignites,
The heart expands as hope excites.
With kisses of aurora on the rise,
A canvas painted across the skies.

All weary souls find solace here,
As daylight whispers, 'Have no fear.'
In morning's glow, our spirits soar,
Kisses of aurora forevermore.

Quenching the Thirst for Dawn

The sky awakens, soft and bright,
Whispers of hope in morning light.
Clouds blush pink, a gentle glow,
As dreams retreat, the day will flow.

Birds stir softly, songs arise,
Chasing away the night's disguise.
Nature sighs, the world is still,
With every breath, time bends to will.

The dew-kissed grass beneath my feet,
Emerald waves, a music sweet.
Sunlight dances on the stream,
Stirring the heart, awakening dream.

A tapestry of colors spread,
Each brush of light, a path we tread.
Morning whispers, secrets shared,
With every moment, love declared.

In the embrace of dawn's soft grace,
A reminder of our sacred space.
We find our peace, our spirit's song,
In the light where we belong.

A Brush of Warm Colors

In a canvas painted wide and true,
Strokes of gold and shades of blue.
The sun dips low, the sky ignites,
A dance of hues, a sweet delight.

Crimson kisses soften the night,
While lavender dreams take gentle flight.
Nature holds her breath in awe,
As evening's brush reveals her law.

Every shadow, a tale untold,
Whispers of warmth in brilliance bold.
The horizon's edge, a fiery seam,
Binding dusk and our shared dream.

A symphony of pigments play,
As day retires, fades into gray.
Painted skies, our souls adore,
In every shade, we long for more.

With twilight's veil, the colors blend,
An artwork that will never end.
In this moment, forever drawn,
We linger here, embracing dawn.

The Silent Fall of Light

As daylight wanes and shadows creep,
A silent world prepares for sleep.
The sun gives way to twilight's grace,
Transforming all in its embrace.

Whispers of dusk, a gentle hush,
Fleeting moments, a calming rush.
Stars awaken, shyly they peep,
In the stillness, thoughts run deep.

The lingering warmth upon the earth,
Bears witness to the day's rebirth.
Faded sunbeams softly fall,
Wrapping everything in night's shawl.

Each breath of wind, a lover's sigh,
The world pauses, a soft goodbye.
In this hour of peaceful retreat,
Nature's rhythm, a heart's heartbeat.

As darkness wraps the sky in lace,
The moon takes her rightful place.
With every star, a dream takes flight,
In the silent fall of light.

Return of the Golden Hour

Here comes the sun with its golden hue,
Waking the world, painting anew.
The air is rich with a soothing balm,
In every breath, a timeless calm.

Fields shimmer under the warming glow,
A moment fleeting, a sacred show.
Life unfolds in a gentle embrace,
Each flower smiles, a radiant face.

Children's laughter fills the air,
Chasing shadows without a care.
Sunset's promise, a fleeting kiss,
In these hours, we find our bliss.

The horizon stretches, colors collide,
A symphony of light, nature's pride.
With every heartbeat, time stands still,
In the golden hour's warm fulfill.

And as the sun dips low to rest,
We gather moments, feeling blessed.
In twilight's glow, dreams start to flower,
Embracing life in the golden hour.

Echoes of Daybreak

As dawn's light begins to rise,
Whispers dance within the skies.
Morning dew on blades of grass,
Time flows on, too swift to pass.

Birds take flight on gentle wings,
Nature wakes and softly sings.
Colors burst in vibrant hues,
A canvas fresh, with morning views.

Sunbeams kiss the sleepy trees,
Rustling softly in the breeze.
Golden rays spread warmth anew,
Painting dreams in shades of blue.

Shadows fade with every note,
Life awakens, hearts devote.
In the silence, echoes play,
A symphony of the day.

Moments linger, softly glide,
In the light, we find our guide.
Echoes call from far and near,
Daybreak's song, forever clear.

Glimmers of Tomorrow

In the hush of twilight's glow,
Whispers tell what we don't know.
Stars begin to wink and shine,
Futures dance on threads of time.

Glimmers spark in night's embrace,
Dreams unfold, a gentle trace.
Through the dark, hope finds a way,
Lighting paths for another day.

Every wish upon a star,
Carries echoes near and far.
In the stillness, hearts do yearn,
For the dreams we seek to learn.

Clouds above may veil the light,
Yet within, we hold the bright.
Glimmers guide us as we strive,
With each challenge, we survive.

Branches reach for skies unknown,
In this journey, we're not alone.
Together we shall face the dawn,
With glimmers of tomorrow drawn.

Between Heaven and Earth

Where mountains rise to touch the sky,
And valleys slope as rivers sigh.
Between the stars and fields so wide,
Lives a world where dreams abide.

Here the sun and moon collide,
In the twilight, love takes stride.
Whispers linger in the air,
Promises of hope laid bare.

Clouds embrace the peaks so high,
Painting stories as they fly.
In the silence, souls connect,
In this space, we introspect.

Raindrops fall on thirsty ground,
In this balance, life is found.
Between the realms, we learn to see,
The beauty in our harmony.

Together we shall build our nest,
In this haven, we find rest.
Between heaven and earth, we'll soar,
With hearts united, forevermore.

Soft Resurgence

When the night begins to fade,
Gentle light our fears invade.
In the hush, resilience speaks,
Awakening the dreams it seeks.

Tender echoes, soft and clear,
Whispering all that we hold dear.
From the ashes, strength will rise,
With new hope, we reach the skies.

Petals bloom in fragrant air,
Each rebirth, a silent prayer.
Nature's pulse beats strong and true,
In every heart, a spark breaks through.

The dawn ignites our hidden ways,
As shadows fade, we find our gaze.
In the light, our spirits dance,
Embracing every fleeting chance.

Soft resurgence, life renewed,
In every moment, love imbued.
With each heartbeat, we reclaim,
The essence of our vivid flame.

The Invitation of Light

In the hush of dawn's embrace,
Shadows wane, the dark will chase.
A gentle whisper calls the day,
Where dreams and hopes begin to play.

Golden rays, a tender glow,
Lift the heart, like wings they flow.
Awakening the world anew,
Inviting life in every hue.

Fragrance of the morning bloom,
Sweeping past each darkened room.
Softly breaking through the night,
We gather close to greet the light.

A dance of spirits, free and bright,
Echoes in the air, pure delight.
The promise of a day so wide,
In light we trust, in joy we bide.

Let the sun's embrace be known,
In every heart, let love be sown.
Together, in this glowing space,
We find our strength, our rightful place.

Radiance at Dusk

The sun dips low, a crimson fire,
Painting skies with deep desire.
Shadows stretch, their tales unfold,
In hues of amber, dreams retold.

Whispers linger in the breeze,
Carrying hopes like autumn leaves.
A soft embrace from twilight's hand,
Where secrets dwell across the land.

Stars awaken, one by one,
Dancing lightly with the sun.
In the stillness, magic brews,
As dusk unfolds her velvet hues.

The world, a canvas, rich and deep,
In radiant shades, the night will weep.
Hearts align as day departs,
While nature sings to yearning hearts.

Beneath the glow of evening's shade,
We find the dreams that time has made.
In this beauty, softly spun,
At dusk, our souls become as one.

Embrace of Twilight

Twilight whispers, softly sighs,
Colors blend across the skies.
The world transforms in gentle grace,
As day gives way to night's embrace.

The stars emerge, a twinkling song,
Nature's rhythm, wild and strong.
Cool breezes carry tender thought,
In silence, peace is gently wrought.

Gathered dreams, like fireflies,
Illuminate the darkened skies.
Each twinkle tells of hopes unseen,
In this moment, we convene.

As shadows grow and daylight wanes,
Softly echoing the past remains.
The moon ascends, a regal sight,
Inviting hearts to dance in light.

With every breath, the night unfolds,
A tapestry of stories told.
In twilight's arms, let worries cease,
And find within a boundless peace.

Where Dreams Meet Daybreak

In the quiet of the morning glow,
Dreams awaken, begin to flow.
Colors paint the waking sky,
Where hopes are born, and spirits fly.

Gentle rays of sunlight stream,
Casting light on every dream.
Whispers of the night take flight,
In the promise of new delight.

The air is fresh, the world anew,
Each heartbeat sings a vibrant hue.
Nature stirs, breaks free from night,
In the warmth of morning's light.

A symphony of life unfolds,
In every moment, courage holds.
The dawn reflects our deepest yearn,
In this place, our souls can learn.

Here we stand at daybreak's gate,
Embracing fate, we celebrate.
With every step, the journey starts,
Where dreams unite and fill our hearts.

Horizon's Hushed Symphony

The sun dips low, a warm embrace,
Painting skies with colors bright.
Whispers in the evening air,
Nature sings, a soft delight.

Waves crash gently on the shore,
A melody of time's own rhyme.
Stars begin to flicker on,
An endless dance, a pulse of time.

The horizon blurs, a fading line,
Where dreams and reality entwine.
A symphony of night unfolds,
In shadows, secrets softly told.

The moon ascends, a silver smile,
Guiding wanderers from afar.
Each note lingers, sweet and soft,
A serenade beneath the stars.

In the stillness, hearts unite,
A world bathed in twilight's hue.
The horizon's song, forever true,
In whispered tones, it welcomes you.

Embracing the Glow

Morning breaks with tender light,
Golden rays that gently flow.
Fields awaken, dew adorned,
Nature's canvas starts to show.

Birds take flight, a joyous song,
Filling hearts with pure delight.
In the warmth of day's embrace,
Every shadow turns to light.

Trees sway softly in the breeze,
Dancing in a rhythmic show.
Each leaf tells a whispered tale,
Of seasons past and time to grow.

Laughter echoes, children play,
In the glow of joyful hours.
Every moment, pure and bright,
A symphony of nature's powers.

As dusk descends, the glow remains,
A lingering warmth in soft twilight.
To embrace this fleeting joy,
Is to cherish life's sweet light.

Chasing Shadows

In twilight's hush, we start to roam,
Seeking secrets hidden near.
Shadows dance beneath the trees,
Fleeting whispers calm our fear.

Footsteps soft on winding paths,
Each turn brings a new surprise.
Mysteries beckon all around,
Underneath the starlit skies.

With every step, a story waits,
In the silence, tales unfold.
Chasing echoes of the past,
In the night, the brave and bold.

The moonlight paints the world in dreams,
Ghostly figures, soft and swift.
Through the dark, we wander free,
In shadows, we find our gift.

Endless journeys yet to take,
In the stillness, hearts aglow.
Chasing shadows, finding light,
In the night, our spirits grow.

Sunkissed Whispers

Beneath the sun, the world awakes,
Awash in warmth, a sweet embrace.
Gentle breezes carry hints,
Of laughter, love, and sacred space.

Golden fields stretch far and wide,
Kissed by sun, they sway and swirl.
In every corner, life will bloom,
Nature's gift, a precious pearl.

Children play with carefree joy,
Chasing dreams on summer's stroll.
Each giggle dances in the sun,
As time unwinds, we lose control.

The horizon glows, a vibrant line,
Where earth and sky converge as one.
Sunkissed whispers, soft and sweet,
Call us home when day is done.

As twilight calls, the sun dips low,
The warmth remains, a tender sigh.
In every ray, the world aglow,
Eternal moments pass us by.

Sun-Kissed Dreams

Golden rays of morning light,
Whisper secrets to the night.
Dancing shadows start to play,
Hopes awaken with the day.

Laughter echoes in the breeze,
Nature hums with rustling leaves.
Every heartbeat sings of grace,
In this bright and cherished space.

Fields of amber stretch so wide,
Underneath the sunlit guide.
Every dream begins to bloom,
Chasing shadows, we make room.

Moments fade but leave a trace,
In our hearts, a warm embrace.
Together we shall find a way,
To weave our dreams by light's array.

As daylight tips to dusk's retreat,
With every star, our journeys meet.
In the glow of twilight's gleam,
We'll nurture our sun-kissed dream.

A Tapestry of Light

Colors blend like threads of fate,
Woven tight, they resonate.
Sparkling moments here and there,
A canvas rich beyond compare.

Brushstrokes dance on evening air,
Filling hearts with vibrant flair.
In the silence, stories weave,
A tapestry that we believe.

Glimmering dreams on every hue,
Infinite in what we pursue.
Each rhythm beats within our soul,
Binding us as we feel whole.

Stars remind us of the night,
In this world, we seek the light.
Hand in hand through every fight,
Creating our own tapestry bright.

Together we'll paint endless skies,
With priceless love that never dies.
As each thread brings us to grace,
We'll cherish this sacred space.

Horizon's Halo

At the cusp where day meets night,
A halo glimmers, pure and bright.
Casting dreams across the shore,
Whispers of what's yet in store.

As waves crash against the sand,
We walk together, hand in hand.
The horizon calls with open arms,
Drawing us near with soothing charms.

Colors bleed into the sky,
Painting wishes as they fly.
In this dance of dusk and dawn,
We find the strength to carry on.

Every sunset brings a tale,
Every memory, precious hail.
Time expands with every beam,
In the warmth of horizon's dream.

Guided by this radiant glow,
We let our inner spirits flow.
In the twilight's gentle grace,
We'll cherish every embrace.

Warmth Beneath the Sky

Underneath this vast expanse,
We gather 'round in joyful dance.
A gentle breeze, a tender sigh,
Wrapped in warmth beneath the sky.

As sunlight kisses all it sees,
Hearts open wide, like blooming trees.
In every laugh, a story shared,
A sprinkle of memories prepared.

Moments linger, sweet and bright,
In the glow of fading light.
Together we shall gaze and sigh,
Finding peace beneath the sky.

With every star, our hopes align,
In this space, your hand in mine.
A world of dreams is ours to fly,
As we bask in what's nearby.

Tomorrow brings a brand new day,
But here and now, we choose to stay.
In the warmth, our spirits high,
Forever anchored, you and I.

Serenade of the Setting Sun

The sky ignites in hues of gold,
A canvas where the day was sold.
Whispers dance in twilight's glow,
As shadows stretch and softly grow.

The birds retreat to nests of peace,
Their serenade begins to cease.
The world exhales a soothing sigh,
Beneath the vast and painted sky.

As dusk wraps tight with tender grace,
Stars emerge, their twinkling face.
A tranquil hush, the day's goodbye,
Embraced by night, the world can lie.

In the distance, waves softly kiss,
Moments drift in quiet bliss.
The sun bows low, a final bow,
Forever etched in heart's sweet vow.

With every sunset holds a dream,
Each fleeting moment, like a stream.
From dusk till dawn, life may begin,
In the glow where hope wears thin.

Warmth Beyond the Waves

The ocean's breath, a soothing balm,
Where gentle tides and hearts find calm.
Golden rays on water's crest,
Nature's lullaby, a sailor's rest.

Children's laughter fills the air,
As footprints leave their tales laid bare.
Seashells whisper stories old,
Secrets of the sea retold.

Beyond the surf, horizons call,
Adventures weave through breezes small.
The sky reflects the ocean's mood,
In colors bright, a vibrant brood.

As dusk descends, the fire glows,
Embers dance in twilight's throes.
Voices blend, both near and far,
Under this vast, eternal star.

With every wave that breaks and swells,
A promise kept, the heart compels.
For in the warmth of sun and sand,
Life's joy is found, hand in hand.

Gilded Horizons

The morning breaks, a golden hue,
Awakening the world anew.
Soft shadows stretch as daylight creeps,
Through slumbered hills where nature sleeps.

Gilded branches, kissed by light,
Dance in harmony, a lovely sight.
Birds take flight on wings of grace,
With every beat, the heart does race.

In fields of gold, dreams come alive,
Bees buzz by, the flowers thrive.
Each petal shines, a burst of cheer,
A fleeting glimpse of love held dear.

As day turns soft with shades of rose,
Whispers linger where the river flows.
Mountains stand with strength and pride,
Guardians where the secrets hide.

With every dusk, horizons gleam,
Life unfolds within a dream.
In every moment, truth bestows,
A tapestry of life that grows.

Twilight's Gentle Kiss

The sky blushes with twilight's grace,
A soft caress, the night's embrace.
Stars awaken, one by one,
In the hush before day is done.

Moonlight drapes the world in peace,
A soothing balm, a sweet release.
Crickets sing their evening song,
While time moves on, both slow and strong.

Each shadow dances on the ground,
In this stillness, hope is found.
Fading light, yet hearts ignite,
In the warmth of the coming night.

As dreams take flight on gentle wings,
The soul awakens to what life brings.
A tranquil heart, the mind at rest,
In twilight's glow, we are truly blessed.

With every kiss of dusk's sweet breath,
Comes a promise beyond our death.
For in the quiet, love endures,
In twilight's arms, our hearts feel pure.

www.ingramcontent.com/pod-product-compliance
Ingram Content Group UK Ltd.
Pitfield, Milton Keynes, MK11 3LW, UK
UKHW031956131224
452403UK00010B/499